Story Cards:

North American Indian Tales

of the
Abnaki, Algonquian, Bella Bella, Brule Sioux,
Cherokee, Cochiti, Coast Salish, Comanche,
Concow Maidu, Cree, Creek, Flathead, Fox, Haida,
Huron-Wyandot, Iroquois, Kalapuya, Kiowa,
Labrador Inuit, Lillooet, Micmac, Nulato, Ojibwa,
Papago, Pima, Pomo, Populaca, Seminole, Seneca, Shasta,
Taos, Tlingit, Winnebago, and Zuñi peoples of the United States,
Canada, and Mexico

Compiled by
Susannah J. Clark

with illustrations by
Ken Rainbow Cougar Edwards

PRO LINGUA ASSOCIATES

BRATTLEBORO, VERMONT

Pro Lingua Associates, Publishers
15 Elm Street
Brattleboro, Vermont 05301 USA

Office 802-257-7779
Orders 800-366-4775
San 216-0579

At Pro Lingua,
our objective is to foster an approach
to learning and teaching that we call
interplay, the **inter**action of language
learners and teachers with their materials,
with the language and culture,
and with each other in active, creative,
and productive **play.**

ISBN 0-86647-083-2

Two percent of the royalties for this book will be contributed on an annual basis to a North American Indian charity.

This book was designed and set by Arthur A. Burrows using Garamond type with Nadianne Book display type. It was printed and bound by BookCrafters of Chelsea, Michigan.

A note about the title of this book: It was our intention from the inception of this project to be respectful to the peoples who are represented by these stories. With this intention, we decided to refer to these peoples as they wish to be referred to. After much consultation with people of various nations all around North America, we determined that, if there is a consensus, it is that these North Americans prefer to be called by the name of their own particular people, be it Abnaki or Zuñi. When a general term is needed, "American Indian" now seems to be preferred by many of the individuals we consulted, though certainly not all.

We wish to express our speical appreciation to Ken Edwards for consulting on several aspects of this book, both as a traditonal storyteller and as a student of North American Indian cultures. His insights and enthusiasm have been invaluable.

First Korean edition printed in South Korea in 1997: **ISBN** 89-86159-19-8 13740

How to Prepare Your Story Cards

These Story Cards come in sheets of four, bound together as a book for ease of handling and to save you money. To prepare the cards for use, follow these easy steps.

1. Tear the pages of cards out of the book; they are perforated at the spine. Cut each sheet in four along the dotted line, trimming the rough edge.

2. These cards are on tough coated stock, but they will last longer if you laminate them.

3. Keep this introductory material in a file for future reference.

Contents

Publisher's Foreword

We at Pro Lingua Associates are pleased to present this collection of North American Indian tales in story card format, following in the footsteps of our *Tales of Nasreddin Hodja* and *Aesop's Fables*. Although our primary purpose continues to be to promote language learning, it is also our pleasure to play a small part in the renewal of interest in the art of storytelling. The time has come for us to rediscover this ancient and very human art form and at the same time break ourselves away from the great storyteller of our age, the television.

We are also proud to offer to our language learners and teachers a collection of folk tales from the earliest inhabitants of the "New World," the North American Indians. Our collection of tales is not intended to be an introduction to the study of the Indians of the North American continent, but if it promotes interest in and further study of these peoples, we will be very pleased.

RCC for PLA

Illustrator's Preface

In traveling across the North American continent, I've come to know how vast the cultural differences are between one tribe and the next. Each has its special designs and use of color. You can't lump all the tribes together and say this is Indian. The tribes are as different as the areas they live in and the animals who share the land with them. In illustrating these stories, I have tried to bring authenticity to the paintings by including in each one some of the unique qualities I have experienced in my personal contacts. I've tried to be accurate in using details of clothing and design. And, of course, the setting of the story is in the natural world of that tribe. The climate, the land, and the animals are appropriate to it.

Storytelling is important to all the Indian people of North America. We have a rich oral history that goes back for thousands of years. These stories are only a small taste of our traditions, for there are multitudes of stories kept alive by the five hundred plus tribes. We love stories–everyone does. As a storyteller, I travel around learning stories and sharing them, particularly with the children. They like these stories about the "animal people." There are many reasons we have kept these and other stories alive. One was that they helped us learn some science and biology, some simple truths about nature and the relations between the animals. Of course, they also helped us understand and solve problems in the relations between people. Another aspect is that through these animal people stories, our children have learned to respect the values and social behavior that are so important to us.

Ken Rainbow Cougar Edwards

North American Indian Peoples of Canada, the United States, and Mexico

whose traditional tales are included in this collection

(The positions shown for tribal territories are only approximate.)

Introduction

These wonderful stories come from the traditions of thirty-four of the hundreds of North American Indian peoples. Like all true folk tales from around the world, these stories have been and are still shared, generation after generation, as a way of passing on wisdom and insights into human nature and the world we live in. These North American Indian stories are especially remarkable as reminders that we humans are very much a part of the natural world, and that the other inhabitants of this world, from mosquitoes to moose, share it with us in ways that may be closer than we think. This collection does not offer a body of wisdom from a single culture. However, you will notice some similarities among the stories. Although the Indian peoples in North America are probably all somewhat related, these thirty-four peoples who live all across North America, from Hudson's Bay in northern Canada to central Mexico, are as varied in language and culture as any on Earth. This suggests that these animal stories have roots that go very deep, and that they have been told with pleasure for a very long time.

Who are these cards designed for?

Anyone studying language arts or English as a second or foreign language will benefit from telling, listening to, reading, and writing these tales. Students with third grade reading skills or advanced beginner language proficiency will be able to use at least the shorter, easier tales. The tales progress from shorter, easier prose to longer, more challenging English.

Because of the prominent role of animal characters, the stories will have great appeal to children, but adults also will enjoy the tales both for language learning and as an introductory exploration of American Indian folklore. This sampling of folklore can also lead to further study of North American Indian cultures.

How many students can use one set of cards?

These cards can be used in a one-on-one tutorial situation. They are very effective for pair work activities. They can also be used by large classes, although it is best to have a set of cards for each eight to ten students, because this will allow you to use the activity several times with your class. Thus, you can have sub-groups each working with a complete set of cards.

Using two sets of cards.

There are advantages to having two sets of cards, even with a small class. (Photocopying for this purpose is not permitted; the illustrations are important.) Two students can work as a pair with the same tale. They can practice telling it to each other while mutually monitoring and prompting each other. They can focus on accuracy as well as fluency. This could be a very good way of preparing for *The Basic Technique* (#1), described in the teaching notes that follow.

Teaching Notes

The basic purpose of this collection is really quite simple. Storytelling is an excellent way for language learners to practice the language they are learning in a holistic way, building linguistic fluency, confidence, and communicative competence as well as gaining insight into the cultures of the storytellers, in this case the original inhabitants of the North American continent, the American Indians.

There are 48 cards in this collection, and on each card is a short tale in clear, modified English. The cards are numbered in the lower right-hand corner, and are ordered from short and easy to longer and more difficult. Therefore, they can be used by a range of learners, from beginning level to advanced. The source of the story is also noted with an S and a number in the lower right-hand corner. The number refers to the list of "sources consulted" on page 6.

This collection of tales on cards is not intended as a primary way to teach *new* linguistic material to learners. The purpose is to stimulate speaking practice, to provide listening practice, and to offer some reading practice. However, it is likely that some new vocabulary will be learned, and some grammatical features can be highlighted. But as these are not primary purposes of these cards, practice exercises are notably absent. Telling a story should be primarily a synthesizing activity, and informative and fun.

1. *The basic technique*

It is quite simple. Give each student in the class a different card. Have them read through the cards silently for comprehension. Circulate and answer questions. Some words may emerge as unknown but necessary to the successful telling of the tale. Take a few minutes to put these words on the board and make sure everybody knows their meaning. With the potentially troublesome vocabulary out of the way, pair the students and have them tell each other their stories. Encourage them to look again at their stories after they have told them, to compare their auditory short-term memory with the story as it is told on the card. They can also show their cards to each other for a brief follow-up reading practice. Then the pair splits up, and they find someone else to share stories with. This continues as many times as you want, although the activity may wear thin after eight exchanges.

There are variations on this technique and other activities that can be done with the cards. A few are suggested below.

2. *Chain Stories.*

Arrange the students in a circle. An even number of students works best. Give a different card to every other student in the circle. The students with the cards tell their tales to the students to their left who are without cards. Then the students who listened turn to the next student in the circle and tell that person the tale, and so on. After all the tales have been told, compare the final versions with the original versions on the card. A variation on this technique is to send a few students out of the room. Bring them in one at a time. Someone in the room tells a tale to the student who comes in. That student tells the tale to the next student who comes in, and so on. Again, compare the final version with the original.

3. *Dictation.*

Dictate a tale to the students, or have pairs of students dictate tales to each other. This is good practice for the punctuation of direct and indirect speech.

4. *Listen and Write.*

Read a tale to the students, and then have them write it out. After they have written it, read it again and let them compare. They can also swap their writings and compare.

5. *Act it out.*

Give a tale to a group of students (one student for each character in the tale plus a narrator) and have them act it out for their classmates.

6. *For the Record.*

After practicing several times, the students take turns making audio or video recordings of their storytelling. Play the tape for the class and for another class, if possible. This activity can be repeated later in the course. By comparing the two tapes, the students should be able to see their progress.

7. *Information Gap Practice.*

Make two enlarged copies of the same tale. White-out two different sets of words on the two cards (six to ten blanks are usually enough). One student begins reading one of the cards and pauses at each missing word. The listener supplies the word and at the same time tries to fill in the words that are missing on their own card. *(Permission is given to photocopy for this kind of activity.)*

About the contributors

The compiler, **Susannah J. Clark,** is a freelance writer and editor living in San Francisco. For Pro Lingua, she was part of the team that developed *The ESL Miscellany*, and she is the co-author of the reader/vocabulary text *Wheels and Wings*. She has worked on the editorial staffs of several magazines, most recently as managing editor of *Giants Magazine,* the publication of San Francisco's baseball team, and she has written for numerous magazines, including *Elle, Decor, Travel & Leisure, Sunset,* and *California Horse Review.* During her research for *North American Indian Tales,* she was startled to find that such thoughtful stories have been largely neglected by modern society. "One thing there can never be too much of is a good story," she says. "An average night in front to the TV just proves the point."

The illustrator, **Ken Rainbow Cougar Edwards**, is a member of the Colville Confederated Tribes from Washington State. He is both an artist and a storyteller. As a student of Indian art and an oral historian, he has travelled extensively in North America to acquire the knowledge and experience necessary in both of these fields. This has taken him to over 60 Indian reservations from as far north as Barrow, Alaska, to as far south as Florida.

Because Ken has learned over a thousand stories from these many different American Indian cultures as well as from his own Colville heritage, he feels that, as he travels as a storyteller, he increases intercultural understanding, both among Indian people and non-Indians. Like any good storyteller, he tailors his stories to fit the age group and the culture of his audience. Sometimes he enhances his storytelling by singing with a drum accompaniment. Sometimes he also shows slides, paintings, or photographs.

As an artist and illustator, Ken works mostly in watercolor and pen and ink. He has done paintings, cards, and posters, as well as book illustations. He writes, "I have always wanted to draw and paint things that no one has ever seen. That is why my style of art is surrealism. Indian spirits and shamans are my favorite subjects. I take many of my ideas from the Indian stories I have learned and put them on canvas or paper, thus showing our people and non-Indians some of the rich culture, traditions, and beliefs that we still have today. I try to find out what I can do, not what I can't do. I like to make people think."

The Cast of Plant and Animal Characters

If your students are not already familiar with these characters, it would be useful to show them pictures or to assign some research before working with the stories. The numbers indicate the story numbers in which each character appears.

Alligator – 7
Ant – 19
Bear – 6, 13, 14, 16, 19, 22, 34
Beaver – 21
Birch - 8
Black Oak – 41
Bluebird – 25
Blue Jay – 11
Buffalo – 4, 32, 48
Butterfly – 44
Buzzard – 38, 42
Cardinal – 47
Cedar – 23
Chickadee – 11
Chipmunk – 14, 22
Corn – 46
Cottonwood – 41
Coyote – 1, 18, 24, 25, 28, 30, 37, 43
Crayfish – 41
Crow – 48
Deer – 2, 28, 43, 47
Dog – 13, 18, 20, 28
Egret – 47
Elm – 3
Frog – 21, 24, 26
Fox – 5, 27
Goose – 5
Grizzly Bear – 33
Ground Squirrel – 33
Gosling – 5
Hare – 15
Hawk – 38
Hawthorne Tree –16
Hemlock – 3
Heron - 47
Jay Bird – 17
Leech – 12
Lizard – 28
Louse – 9
Meadow Lark – 38
Mockingbird – 43
Mole – 36
Moose – 8, 26
Mosquito – 10, 45
Mouse – 43
Norway Pine – 10
Oak – 3
Owl – 47
Panther – 47
Pine – 3
Possum – 42
Porcupine – 16, 22
Rabbit – 29, 47
Raccoon – 26, 41
Raven – 11, 35
Redheaded Woodpecker – 42
Robin – 11
Snake – 30
Spider – 42
Squirrel – 38
Strawberry – 1
Swan – 47
Turkey – 29, 30
Wildcat – 29
Willow – 41
Wolf – 16, 18
Wood Tick – 37
Yellowjacket – 19

Storyteller Ken Rainbow Cougar Edwards provided information on the traditional genders of the characters in these stories. He explains that some stories are specifically about female animals, some about male. In this case, gender specific terms like buck and doe may be used. Often you can tell the sex of an animal character because it is doing work traditionally done by a man or a woman in that culture. Hunters are generally male, for example. When the gender is unimportant, the storyteller will often avoid being specific, allowing the listener to decide. However, certain animals are always male–Coyote, for example, and Raven. Others, like Wolf and Buffalo, tend to be male. The land or Earth is always female in all the cultures Mr. Edwards has studied, and the Creator or Great Spirit, who is known by many names, is always male, even in matriarchal societies like the Seneca and the Iroquois.

Useful Resources

for further exploration of North American Indian Cultures

Bierhorst, John. *Mythology of Mexico and Central America.* New York: William Morrow, 1992.
Bruchac, Joseph, and Michael J. Caduto. *Keepers of the Earth.* Golden, Colorado: Fulcrum Inc., 1989.
Bruchac, Joseph, and Michael J. Caduto. *Keepers of the Earth, Teacher's Guide/audiocassettes.* Golden, Colorado: Fulcrum Inc., 1988.
Bruchac, Joseph. *Native American Stories (* from *Keepers of the Earth).* Golden, Colorado: Fulcrum Inc., 1992.
Bruchac, Joseph, and Michael J. Caduto. *Keepers of the Animals.* Golden, Colorado: Fulcrum Inc., 1989.
Bruchac, Joseph, and Michael J. Caduto. *Keepers of the Animals, Teacher's Guide/audiocassettes.* Golden, Colorado: Fulcrum Inc., 1988.
Bruchac, Joseph. *Native American Animal Stories (*from *Keepers of the Animals).* Golden, Colorado: Fulcrum Inc., 1992.
Erdoes, Richard and Ortiz, Alfonso. *American Indian Myths and Legends.* New York: Pantheon Books, 1984.
Simmons, William S. *Spirit of the New England Tribes, Indian History and Folklore, 1620-1984.* Hanover, N.H.: University Press of New England, 1986.
Snyder, Fred. *Native American Directory: Alaska, Canada, and U.S..* San Carlos, Arizona: National Native American Co-Operative, 1982.
Storm, Hyemeyohsts. *Seven Arrows.* New York: Ballantine Books, 1972.
Robinson, Barbara. *Native American Source Book: A Teacher's Resource on New England Native Peoples.* Concord, Mass.:Concord Museum, 1988.

Sources Consulted

1. Adamson, Thelma. "Folk Tales of the Coast Salish." *American Folklore Society* vol. 27, 1934.
2. Barnouw, Victor. *Wisconsin Chippewa Myths and Tales*. Madison, Wisconsin: University of Wisconsin Press, 1977.
3. Boas, Franz. "Bella Bella Tales." *American Folklore Society* vol. 25, 1932.
4. Chapman, John W. "Ten'a Texts and Tales." *American Ethnological Society* vol. 6, 1914.
5. Clark, Cora and Williams, Texa Bowen. *Pomo Indian Myths*. New York: Vintage Press, 1954.
6. Clark, Ella Elizabeth. *Indian Legends of Canada*. Toronto: McClelland and Stewart, Ltd., 1960.
7. Curtin, Jeremiah. *Seneca Indian Myths*. New York: E.P.Dutton & Co., 1923.
8. Curtis, Natalie. *The Indians' Book.* New York: Dover Publications, 1950.
9. Erdoes, Richard and Ortiz, Alfonso. *American Indian Myths and Legends.* New York: Pantheon Books, 1984.
10. Foster, George M. "Sierra Populaca Folklore and Beliefs." *American Archaeology and Ethnology* vol. 42, no. 2. Berkeley and Los Angeles, California: University of California Press, 1945.
11. Jewell, Donald P. *Indians of the Feather River: Tales and Legends of Concow Maidu of California.* Menlo Park, California: Ballena Press, 1987.
12. Marriott, Alice and Rachlin, Carol K. *American Indian Mythology.* New York: Thomas Y. Crowell Co.,1968.
13. Parsons, Elsie Clews. "Taos Tales." *American Folklore Society* vol. 34, 1940.
14. Stevens, James. *Sacred Legends of the Sandy Lake Cree*. Toronto/Montreal: McClelland and Stewart, Ltd., 1971.
15. Swanton, John R. *Myths and Tales of the Southeastern Indians.* Washington, D.C.: Smithsonian Institution, Bureau of American Ethnology, Bulletin 88, 1929.
16. Thompson, Stith. *Tales of the North American Indians*. Bloomington, Indiana: Indiana University Press, 1929.

Other Story Card Collections Available

Pro Lingua Associates has two other collections: ***Story Cards: Aesop's Fables*** by Raymond C. Clark, with illustrations by Hannah Bonner, and ***Story Cards: Tales of Nasreddin Hodja*** also by Raymond C. Clark, with illustrations by Robert MacLean.

Why Deer Stares

Bella Bella

STORY CARDS: NORTH AMERICAN INDIAN TALES
by Susannah J. Clark, illustrated by Ken Rainbow Cougar Edwards
PRO LINGUA ASSOCIATES
15 Elm Street, Brattleboro, Vermont 05301 USA 800-366-4775

The Creation of Strawberries

Concow Maidu

STORY CARDS: NORTH AMERICAN INDIAN TALES
by Susannah J. Clark, illustrated by Ken Rainbow Cougar Edwards
PRO LINGUA ASSOCIATES
15 Elm Street, Brattleboro, Vermont 05301 USA 800-366-4775
Copyright © 1995 by Susannah J. Clark

Why Buffalo Has a Hump

Ojibwa

STORY CARDS: NORTH AMERICAN INDIAN TALES
by Susannah J. Clark, illustrated by Ken Rainbow Cougar Edwards
PRO LINGUA ASSOCIATES
15 Elm Street, Brattleboro, Vermont 05301 USA 800-366-4775
Copyright © 1995 by Susannah J. Clark

Hemlock

Seneca

STORY CARDS: NORTH AMERICAN INDIAN TALES
by Susannah J. Clark, illustrated by Ken Rainbow Cougar Edwards
PRO LINGUA ASSOCIATES
15 Elm Street, Brattleboro, Vermont 05301 USA 800-366-4775
Copyright © 1995 by Susannah J. Clark

The Creation of Strawberries

Concow Maidu

The Creator was making an unusual fruit when Coyote came along. "What are you doing?" he asked.

"I am making a special fruit for old people," the Creator said. "It has no seeds to get caught in their teeth."

Coyote thought this was funny. "All fruit has seeds," he said, and just as the Creator finished making the fruit, Coyote threw a handful of small seeds. They stuck on the skin of the fruit. That is why the strawberry's seeds are on the outside.

1 (S:11)

Why Deer Stares

Bella Bella

Deer was burning the outside of his canoe to clean it. Some people who were camped across the river started dancing, and Deer began to watch. He became so interested in the dance that he forgot to pay attention to his canoe, which caught fire. The dancers called to Deer, "Your canoe is burning," but Deer kept watching the dance, and his canoe burned to ashes. Ever since that time, Deer has no canoe, and when he sees people, he watches them and pays no attention to anything else.

2 (S:3)

Hemlock

Seneca

The trees were arguing about which of them was the strongest. First the oak tree said it was the strongest. Then the elm tree said it was. But one young pine tree boasted louder than any of the others that it was stronger than all the other trees. A very old pine tree became angry with its nephew. "You think you are so strong?" it asked. The old pine pressed down on the young tree's head so hard that the young tree shrank, and its branches crowded together. Now we call the young tree Hemlock, and it does not grow so tall.

3 (S:7)

Why Buffalo Has a Hump

Ojibwa

Buffalo loved to run across the prairie. One day he ran to a place where the ground birds built their nests. They screamed at Buffalo because he was trampling their children, but he kept runnning and did not stop.

Suddenly the Great Spirit appeared. He beat Buffalo on the shoulders with a stick, but Buffalo just humped up his shoulders so he would not feel the blows. Buffalo's arrogance angered the Great Spirit, who shouted, "From now on you will always carry a hump on your shoulders, and you will carry your head low in shame for your unkindness to the birds."

4 (S:6)

Bear Loses Its Tail

Coast Salish

STORY CARDS: NORTH AMERICAN INDIAN TALES
by Susannah J. Clark, illustrated by Ken Rainbow Cougar Edwards
PRO LINGUA ASSOCIATES
15 Elm Street, Brattleboro, Vermont 05301 USA 800-366-4775

How Fox Became Red

Nulato

STORY CARDS: NORTH AMERICAN INDIAN TALES
by Susannah J. Clark, illustrated by Ken Rainbow Cougar Edwards
PRO LINGUA ASSOCIATES
15 Elm Street, Brattleboro, Vermont 05301 USA 800-366-4775
Copyright © 1995 by Susannah J. Clark

Moose

Abnaki

STORY CARDS: NORTH AMERICAN INDIAN TALES
by Susannah J. Clark, illustrated by Ken Rainbow Cougar Edwards
PRO LINGUA ASSOCIATES
15 Elm Street, Brattleboro, Vermont 05301 USA 800-366-4775
Copyright © 1995 by Susannah J. Clark

Why Alligator Has No Tongue

Populaca

STORY CARDS: NORTH AMERICAN INDIAN TALES
by Susannah J. Clark, illustrated by Ken Rainbow Cougar Edwards
PRO LINGUA ASSOCIATES
15 Elm Street, Brattleboro, Vermont 05301 USA 800-366-4775
Copyright © 1995 by Susannah J. Clark

How Fox Became Red

Nulato

Fox was hunting one day when he saw a fat goose and her goslings walking beside the lake. Fox was very hungry. He crept closer to the geese. Fox said to himself, "Now I will have a tasty dinner!"

Suddenly he jumped out of the trees and ran at the geese, but they were quicker than Fox. They jumped into the water and swam away.

Fox was very angry that the geese had escaped. He walked beside the water and watched them swim away. The geese laughed at him. Fox became very angry and turned bright red all over. Only the tip of his tail, which fell into the water, remained white.

Bear Loses Its Tail

Coast Salish

One winter Bear was asleep in its cave when a warm afternoon woke it. Bear decided to go to the frozen lake to enjoy the sun. It walked to the middle of the lake and sat down on the ice. The warm sun began to melt the ice. The sun was so warm that it made Bear feel sleepy again, and it fell asleep. A few hours later, the sun went down, and it began to get cold again. The chill in the air finally woke Bear. It jumped up quickly to run back to its warm cave, but its tail was frozen in the ice. And that's how Bear lost its long tail.

Why Alligator Has No Tongue

Populaca

A hunter was walking along the edge of a river when he met Alligator. Alligator said to the man, "You woke me from my nap, and now I am going to kill you."

The man thought quickly and asked Alligator, "How are you going to kill me?"

"Like this," Alligator said, and he thrashed his body back and forth, beat his tail on the ground, and snapped his jaws. Suddenly the man picked up a large stone and threw it into Alligator's mouth, propping it open. Alligator was so surprised that he stopped thrashing. Quickly the man pulled out his knife and cut off Alligator's tongue. To this day Alligator still has no tongue.

Moose

Abnaki

Once Moose was so large that he ate the tops of trees. He did not always look where he was going, and sometimes he stepped on smaller animals and killed them. So the Great Spirit went to make Moose smaller. He took a strip of birch bark three hands long and rolled it into a horn. He blew into the horn, and soon Moose appeared. "I have come to make you smaller so that you will no longer hurt my children," He said.

The Great Spirit took Moose's horns and pushed him down to the size that he is today. Now Moose is no longer as dangerous, and to this day, the hunter calls him with a horn of birch bark.

Mosquito and Lightning

Ojibwa

STORY CARDS: NORTH AMERICAN INDIAN TALES
by Susannah J. Clark, illustrated by Ken Rainbow Cougar Edwards
PRO LINGUA ASSOCIATES
15 Elm Street, Brattleboro, Vermont 05301 USA 800-366-4775

Why Salt Man Went Away

Zuñi

STORY CARDS: NORTH AMERICAN INDIAN TALES
by Susannah J. Clark, illustrated by Ken Rainbow Cougar Edwards
PRO LINGUA ASSOCIATES
15 Elm Street, Brattleboro, Vermont 05301 USA 800-366-4775
Copyright © 1995 by Susannah J. Clark

Respect

Ojibwa

STORY CARDS: NORTH AMERICAN INDIAN TALES
by Susannah J. Clark, illustrated by Ken Rainbow Cougar Edwards
PRO LINGUA ASSOCIATES
15 Elm Street, Brattleboro, Vermont 05301 USA 800-366-4775
Copyright © 1995 by Susannah J. Clark

Why Raven Is Black

Bella Bella

STORY CARDS: NORTH AMERICAN INDIAN TALES
by Susannah J. Clark, illustrated by Ken Rainbow Cougar Edwards
PRO LINGUA ASSOCIATES
15 Elm Street, Brattleboro, Vermont 05301 USA 800-366-4775
Copyright © 1995 by Susannah J. Clark

Why Salt Man Went Away

Zuñi

Salt Man and Louse were talking. "The people are very fond of me," Salt Man said. "They always use me to make their food taste better."

Louse replied, "I am closer to the people than you are. Every day they carry me with them. At the dances I tickle them and make them itch. I am always in their hair and in their clothes, even their best ones. So you see, Salt Man, you are important to the people, but you are with them only at meals. I am with them all the time."

Salt Man thought this meant the people liked Louse better than him. He became very sad, so he went to live in the south. That is why there are no salt mines near the Zuñi people.

9 (S:13)

Mosquito and Lightning

Ojibwa

One day Mosquito stopped to rest on the top of a Norway pine tree. It had just eaten, and was fat and full of blood. Lightning, who was very thin, saw Mosquito's fat red belly and asked, "Mosquito, what do you eat that makes you so fat?"

Mosquito did not want to share its food, so it showed Lightning a bit of pitch from the top of the pine tree. "This is what I eat, Lightning," it said.

Lightning wanted to be fat like Mosquito. It decided to taste the pitch, but when it tried, it split the top of the tree. It was not discouraged, though, and it tried again and again. To this day it is still trying to eat Norway pine pitch, and that is why so many Norway pine trees have been struck by lightning.

10 (S:2)

Why Raven Is Black

Bella Bella

The birds met one day to dance. First, they painted themselves with beautiful colors. Robin painted on a red breast. Chickadee painted a black cap. Blue Jay painted his wings blue. All the birds painted themselves in beautiful patterns except Raven. He just sat and watched. "I don't want to play your silly games," he said when the other birds asked him to join in.

So the birds left Raven alone and got ready to dance. They beat their drums and sang. As each bird did its dance, Raven became more interested. Finally he jumped up and said, "Let me dance, too!"

The other birds told Raven he had to paint himself first, but all the paint had been used up except a little black paint. So Raven painted himself with what was left, and that is how he got his color.

11 (S:3)

Respect

Ojibwa

Two women were paddling their canoe on a lake. "This is Leech Lake," the first woman said to the second. We must pay our respects to Leech." The first woman took off all her beads and put them into the lake.

The second woman laughed. "I am not going to put my beads in the lake," she said. "I want to keep my beads. I do not need to pay respect to silly little Leech." Suddenly the two women saw a giant leech two feet wide swimming towards them. The second woman quickly tried to take her beads off, but it was too late. Leech bumped the canoe and knocked the woman into the lake. It wrapped itself around her and carried her to the bottom, where she drowned. That is why Indians have respect for all things, even things that seem small and insignificant.

12 (S:2)

How Chipmunk Got Her Stripes

Seneca

STORY CARDS: NORTH AMERICAN INDIAN TALES
by Susannah J. Clark, illustrated by Ken Rainbow Cougar Edwards
PRO LINGUA ASSOCIATES
15 Elm Street, Brattleboro, Vermont 05301 USA 800-366-4775

The Origin of the Big Dipper

Fox

STORY CARDS: NORTH AMERICAN INDIAN TALES
by Susannah J. Clark, illustrated by Ken Rainbow Cougar Edwards
PRO LINGUA ASSOCIATES
15 Elm Street, Brattleboro, Vermont 05301 USA 800-366-4775
Copyright © 1995 by Susannah J. Clark

How Porcupine Got Her Quills

Ojibwa

STORY CARDS: NORTH AMERICAN INDIAN TALES
by Susannah J. Clark, illustrated by Ken Rainbow Cougar Edwards
PRO LINGUA ASSOCIATES
15 Elm Street, Brattleboro, Vermont 05301 USA 800-366-4775
Copyright © 1995 by Susannah J. Clark

The Hare and the Sun

Winnebago

STORY CARDS: NORTH AMERICAN INDIAN TALES
by Susannah J. Clark, illustrated by Ken Rainbow Cougar Edwards
PRO LINGUA ASSOCIATES
15 Elm Street, Brattleboro, Vermont 05301 USA 800-366-4775
Copyright © 1995 by Susannah J. Clark

The Origin of the Big Dipper

Fox

Three men decided to hunt Bear. One of the men brought his little dog, Hold Tight. When they found a bear's cave, Hold Tight ran into it and chased the bear outside. The hunters tried to shoot the bear, but it was too fast for them and ran north. The hunters chased it and chased it, but they couldn't catch up with it.

Finally one of the hunters looked down and saw that the earth was far below them. "Oh, no!" the man shouted. "The bear is leading us up into the sky! Let's go back before it's too late!" But it was already too late, and the hunters were trapped in the sky. You can see them there today, still chasing the bear. Four stars in a square are the bear, the three stars behind it are the hunters, and the tiny little star, the one you can hardly see, is Hold Tight, the dog.

13 (S:12)

How Chipmunk Got Her Stripes

Seneca

Bear thought he was the strongest animal in the forest and always went around saying this to all the other animals. Finally Chipmunk became tired of Bear's bragging. "You are not so strong," she said.

Bear shook his head. "I am the strongest animal there is," he said.

"Prove it," said Chipmunk. "If you are so strong, stop the sun from rising tomorrow."

"Wait and see," Bear said. All the animals sat up that night with Bear and Chipmunk to see if Bear could stop the sun from rising. The next morning, however, the sun rose as usual. All the animals laughed at Bear, but Chipmunk laughed loudest. She laughed so hard that Bear became very angry and chased Chipmunk all the way home. Chipmunk was just squeezing into her hole when Bear reached out and scratched Chipmunk across the back with his big paw. To this day, Chipmunk wears the marks from Bear's claws on her back.

14 (S:7)

The Hare and the Sun

Winnebago

One day, Hare found a trail where some huge thing had passed by. "I must find out what this is," he said, so he blocked the trail with trees and stones.

The next day he went back to the trail and saw that something had crashed through the trees and stones. So Hare made a large net and spread it across the trail. The next day when Hare returned, he found the sun, who used the trail every day, struggling to get free. Hare was very frightened, because he knew his people could not live unless the sun did its work every day. Hare tried to untie the net, but the sun was so hot that Hare could not face it. Hare could only keep his back to the sun, with his face turned away. Even so, his hind parts were so badly burned that to this day, the skin of the rabbit's hindquarters is tender and easily broken.

15 (S:8)

How Porcupine Got Her Quills

Ojibwa

Porcupine was always hiding from Bear, who loved to eat her. Then one day when she was hiding under a hawthorne tree, she noticed the prickly branches, and she got an idea. Porcupine broke off some of the branches and stuck them onto her back. Bear came near, and as usual he tried to catch Porcupine, but this time he got a paw full of sharp hawthorne spines and ran home, crying.

The Creator saw what had happened and said to Porcupine, "That is a very clever trick you played on Bear." He took some of the branches and peeled the bark off them so they were white. Then He put some clay on Porcupine's back and stuck the quills in them. "Let's see how that works," He said.

Soon Wolf came along. Porcupine rolled herself into a little ball. Wolf tried to take a bite but ran home, howling. And that is how porcupines got their quills.

16 (S:6)

Wolf, Coyote, and Dog

Coast Salish

STORY CARDS: NORTH AMERICAN INDIAN TALES
by Susannah J. Clark, illustrated by Ken Rainbow Cougar Edwards
PRO LINGUA ASSOCIATES
15 Elm Street, Brattleboro, Vermont 05301 USA 800-366-4775

Old Salt Woman

Cochiti

STORY CARDS: NORTH AMERICAN INDIAN TALES
by Susannah J. Clark, illustrated by Ken Rainbow Cougar Edwards
PRO LINGUA ASSOCIATES
15 Elm Street, Brattleboro, Vermont 05301 USA 800-366-4775
Copyright © 1995 by Susannah J. Clark

Why Dogs Don't Talk

Cree

STORY CARDS: NORTH AMERICAN INDIAN TALES
by Susannah J. Clark, illustrated by Ken Rainbow Cougar Edwards
PRO LINGUA ASSOCIATES
15 Elm Street, Brattleboro, Vermont 05301 USA 800-366-4775
Copyright © 1995 by Susannah J. Clark

Day and Night

Coast Salish

STORY CARDS: NORTH AMERICAN INDIAN TALES
by Susannah J. Clark, illustrated by Ken Rainbow Cougar Edwards
PRO LINGUA ASSOCIATES
15 Elm Street, Brattleboro, Vermont 05301 USA 800-366-4775
Copyright © 1995 by Susannah J. Clark

Old Salt Woman

Cochiti

Once, before people used salt in their food, Old Salt Woman was hungry and poor. She came to a village and asked for food, but no one would give her any. Finally she came to a place outside the pueblo where all the children were playing. She showed them a giant salt crystal, and they were fascinated. They followed her out of the village, and there she changed them into jay birds.

Salt Woman went to another village, but there she was treated well and fed. "I am grateful for your kindness," she told the people, and she gave them some of her crystals. She told them to put the crystals on their bread and meat, and when they did, their food tasted better. "I am going to the southeast," she said. "Whenever you want more of my crystals, come to me." She left the village and went to Salt Lake, and so the Cochiti Indians always go there to gather salt.

Wolf, Coyote, and Dog

Coast Salish

Wolf, Coyote, and Dog are brothers. They lived together once, and they kept their camp fire burning all the time. But one day, when they were out hunting, their fire went out.

"Which one of us will go ask the people for some fire?" Wolf asked.

"I will," said Dog.

Dog's brothers did not like people. They were glad they did not have to go. "All right," they said.

So Dog went to the people's camp to ask for fire. But when he got there, the people liked Dog very much. They petted him and gave him something to eat. They did not want him to leave. "Live with us," they said. "We'll take care of you, and you'll never have to hunt again." Dog liked the people, and he decided to stay with them. He never went home again, and even today Dog's brothers are still angry with him for leaving them. When Wolf and Coyote meet Dog, they always fight.

Day and Night

Coast Salish

Bear, Ant, and Yellowjacket were arguing about how long day and night should be. Bear, who liked to sleep, said, "Day and night should each last for six months– one day and one night in each year." But Ant and Yellowjacket wanted day and night to be much shorter– many days and nights in a year.

The three decided to have a race, and the winner would decide the length of day and night. They began the race, and Bear took the lead. However, Ant quickly whispered something to Yellowjacket, who caught up to Bear and began to sting him. Bear was confused by the stings and climbed up a tree. Meanwhile, Ant won the race, and that is why we have many days and nights in a year.

But Bear is still angry because Ant and Yellowjacket tricked him, so he stubbornly sleeps for three months at a time. And he tears up the nests of Ant and Yellowjacket whenever he can find them.

Why Dogs Don't Talk

Cree

A long time ago, animals could talk as well as people. In one village, the dogs began to complain that the people did not treat them well. They had to pull heavy sleds all day. At night they had to sleep outdoors in the cold snow. They did not get very much to eat, and some dogs were beaten. "We work hard, but we are treated badly," the dogs said to each other.

They called a pow-wow. They talked about their problems and tried to decide how to solve them. Then one old dog spoke up. "Be grateful for what you have. Yesterday I heard my master say that soon he will send one of his dogs to carry a message to his relatives many miles away. If all the people make us carry messages, we will never see our families."

The dogs were frightened. They decided they would stop talking so they would not have to carry messages. To this day, dogs still don't talk.

Night and Day

Iroquois

STORY CARDS: NORTH AMERICAN INDIAN TALES
by Susannah J. Clark, illustrated by Ken Rainbow Cougar Edwards
PRO LINGUA ASSOCIATES
15 Elm Street, Brattleboro, Vermont 05301 USA 800-366-4775

Man in the Moon

Lillooet

STORY CARDS: NORTH AMERICAN INDIAN TALES
by Susannah J. Clark, illustrated by Ken Rainbow Cougar Edwards
PRO LINGUA ASSOCIATES
15 Elm Street, Brattleboro, Vermont 05301 USA 800-366-4775
Copyright © 1995 by Susannah J. Clark

Coyote Takes Water from the Frogs

Kalapuya

STORY CARDS: NORTH AMERICAN INDIAN TALES
by Susannah J. Clark, illustrated by Ken Rainbow Cougar Edwards
PRO LINGUA ASSOCIATES
15 Elm Street, Brattleboro, Vermont 05301 USA 800-366-4775
Copyright © 1995 by Susannah J. Clark

The Origin of Cedar Trees

Haida

STORY CARDS: NORTH AMERICAN INDIAN TALES
by Susannah J. Clark, illustrated by Ken Rainbow Cougar Edwards
PRO LINGUA ASSOCIATES
15 Elm Street, Brattleboro, Vermont 05301 USA 800-366-4775
Copyright © 1995 by Susannah J. Clark

Man in the Moon

Lillooet

Beaver fell in love with the three Frog sisters. He went to the swamp where they lived. "Will one of you marry me?" he asked them. But the three Frog sisters were mean, and they laughed at Beaver and called him names. Beaver was so heart-broken that he ran home and cried for days.

He cried so much that his tears flooded the Frog sisters' swamp. They had to find a safe place from the flood, so they swam to Beaver's house and asked if they could come in. But Beaver remembered the names they had called him and told them to go away. He cried harder, and a stream of his tears carried the frogs away.

As they were floating past Moon's house, he looked out and saw them. He felt sorry for them, so he invited them in. The Frog sisters were so grateful they leaped up to kiss his face. When you look at Moon today you can see they are kissing him still.

21 (S:16)

Night and Day

Iroquois

Once the porcupine was the leader of all animals. She gathered everyone together to ask them how long day and night should be. This was a very important question, and soon all the animals began to argue. Chipmunk thought that day and night should each be very short. Bear thought day and night should be very long. They argued for many hours, but they could not agree.

Finally, Chipmunk and Bear decided to have a contest. They each sang songs to the sun and the moon. Chipmunk sang, calling the sun and moon to come often. Bear sang about long days and nights. He asked the sun to sleep for a long time. But the sun began to wake up. Bear understood that the sun liked chipmunk's song better. Bear became very angry and chased Chipmunk all the way home. Just as Chipmunk was going into her hole, Bear swiped his huge paw down Chipmunk's back. This is why the Chipmunk has stripes on her back and why we have short days and nights.

22 (S:16)

The Origin of Cedar Trees

Haida

After the world was made, the Creator put the Haida Indians on the land that is now called the Queen Charlotte Islands. "This is a good place. You will be happy here," the Creator said. But soon the Haidas began to quarrel and fight. The Creator came back to the Haidas and said, "If you cannot live together in peace, I will punish you." The Haidas promised they would live happily ever after, but it did not take long before they were arguing again.

The Creator came again and told the Haidas, "You knew I would punish you if you could not live in peace." Instantly He changed all the people into cedar trees. "Now when people come to these islands, they will see you and remember what happens when you cannot live in peace."

But from evil comes good. The Haidas who came later to the islands used the cedar trees to build houses and canoes. From the roots they made baskets and mats, and from the bark fibers they wove clothing.

23 (S:6)

Coyote Takes Water from the Frogs

Kalapuya

Once the frogs owned all the water. They kept it behind a dam, and if anyone wanted to wash or drink, they had to bring a present to the frogs. Coyote went to see the frogs. "I would like a drink," he said, and he gave them a beautiful shell.

"You may drink," they answered, and Coyote put his head in the water.

After a few minutes, one of the frogs said, "You are taking a long time, Coyote."

"I am very thirsty," Coyote answered. "Let me drink."

After a while another frog spoke. "I think you should give us another shell. You are taking a very long drink."

"I will," Coyote answered. "As soon as I am through."

Finally the frogs became suspicious. "Coyote is doing something," they said. They were right – Coyote was digging a tunnel underneath the dam. Suddenly the dam collapsed, and the water rushed out. It ran into the rivers and lakes and oceans, where it remains today. And no one needs to bring a present when they want a drink.

24 (S:9)

Four Months of Winter

Cree

STORY CARDS: NORTH AMERICAN INDIAN TALES
by Susannah J. Clark, illustrated by Ken Rainbow Cougar Edwards
PRO LINGUA ASSOCIATES
15 Elm Street, Brattleboro, Vermont 05301 USA 800-366-4775
Copyright © 1995 by Susannah J. Clark

Bluebird and Coyote

Pima

STORY CARDS: NORTH AMERICAN INDIAN TALES
by Susannah J. Clark, illustrated by Ken Rainbow Cougar Edwards
PRO LINGUA ASSOCIATES
15 Elm Street, Brattleboro, Vermont 05301 USA 800-366-4775
Copyright © 1995 by Susannah J. Clark

The Lizard Hand

Pomo

STORY CARDS: NORTH AMERICAN INDIAN TALES
by Susannah J. Clark, illustrated by Ken Rainbow Cougar Edwards
PRO LINGUA ASSOCIATES
15 Elm Street, Brattleboro, Vermont 05301 USA 800-366-4775
Copyright © 1995 by Susannah J. Clark

Why Fox Does Not Like Humans

Labrador Eskimo

STORY CARDS: NORTH AMERICAN INDIAN TALES
by Susannah J. Clark, illustrated by Ken Rainbow Cougar Edwards
PRO LINGUA ASSOCIATES
15 Elm Street, Brattleboro, Vermont 05301 USA 800-366-4775
Copyright © 1995 by Susannah J. Clark

Bluebird and Coyote

Pima

Once Bluebird was a dull gray color. She went to a magic lake and bathed in the water, singing, "Blue water, make me blue." When she came out of the water, she was a beautiful shade of blue.

At that time Coyote was bright green. Coyote saw Bluebird's new color and decided he wanted to be blue, too. Bluebird told Coyote how to become blue, but she also said, "You must be careful after you come out of the lake, because the color does not dry until the next day."

Coyote followed Bluebird's instructions, and when he came out of the lake, he was as blue as the bird. Coyote was very proud of his new color. As he walked along, he turned up his nose at all the plain-colored animals who stopped to watch him go by. With his face in the air, he did not see a rock in the road. Coyote tripped and fell in the dust. The dust covered his blue fur and made it the color of dirt. To this day he is still that color.

Four Months of Winter

Cree

The Creator had to make a decision. He called the animals together to help Him decide. "How long should winter be?" He asked them.

Huge old Moose spoke up. "Winter should have as many months as there are hairs on my body."

The animals respected Moose, so they nodded in agreement. But the Creator said, "There will be snow and ice for centuries if I make winter that long."

Next, Raccoon said, "Winter should have as many months as there are teeth in my head."

The animals liked friendly Raccoon, so they nodded in agreement. But again, the Creator shook His head. "Many animals will suffer and die if I make winter that long."

Then Frog spoke up. "Winter should have as many months as there are toes on my foot."

The animals did not respect or like this ugly creature who lived in the mud. They laughed at its suggestion. But the Creator said, "Frog is right. That is a good length for winter." And so winter has four months, just as Frog has four toes.

Why Fox Does Not Like Humans

Labrador Inuit

A man who lived by himself came home from hunting one day. His house was clean, and a pot of stew was bubbling over the fire. But he could not find who had done it. There was no sign that anyone had been there except a very strong, unpleasant smell. From that day on, every time the man came home, he found his house cleaned and his supper waiting.

One day he decided to find out who was doing it. He pretended to go hunting but hid nearby instead. Before too long he saw Fox enter his house. He went back inside his house and found Fox preparing dinner.

"Do you like the food I cook for you while you are away?" Fox asked.

"I like it very much," the man answered. "But what is that strong smell that is always here when you leave?"

"If you do not like the way I smell," Fox said, "I will not bother you any more." She ran from the house, and since then, Humans must cook their own meals, and Fox avoids them whenever she can.

The Lizard Hand

Pomo

When Coyote was creating humans, he needed advice. He called all the animals together. "I can't decide what kind of hand to give humans," he said.

Dog held up his paw. "I think they should have a hand like mine. It is good for running long distances."

Deer held up his hoof. "I think my hand is better," he said. "It is good for climbing to high places."

All the animals agreed that Dog and Deer had very practical hands. Then Lizard spoke up. "It is true that Dog's and Deer's hands are very useful. But humans will not need a hand that is good for running long distances. They will not need a hand that is good for climbing to high places." Lizard held up his own graceful hand. "No, Coyote, humans should have a hand like mine. With this hand, they will be able to do many things. A hand like Deer's or Dog's would not be of much use at all."

"That is true," Coyote agreed. "The lizard hand is best." So that is why humans have a useful hand like Lizard's.

The Origin of Snakes

Taos

STORY CARDS: NORTH AMERICAN INDIAN TALES
by Susannah J. Clark, illustrated by Ken Rainbow Cougar Edwards
PRO LINGUA ASSOCIATES
15 Elm Street, Brattleboro, Vermont 05301 USA 800-366-4775

Rabbit's Tail

Creek

STORY CARDS: NORTH AMERICAN INDIAN TALES
by Susannah J. Clark, illustrated by Ken Rainbow Cougar Edwards
PRO LINGUA ASSOCIATES
15 Elm Street, Brattleboro, Vermont 05301 USA 800-366-4775
Copyright © 1995 by Susannah J. Clark

Why Buffalo Went Away

Kiowa

STORY CARDS: NORTH AMERICAN INDIAN TALES
by Susannah J. Clark, illustrated by Ken Rainbow Cougar Edwards
PRO LINGUA ASSOCIATES
15 Elm Street, Brattleboro, Vermont 05301 USA 800-366-4775
Copyright © 1995 by Susannah J. Clark

Seven Stars

Huron-Wyandot

STORY CARDS: NORTH AMERICAN INDIAN TALES
by Susannah J. Clark, illustrated by Ken Rainbow Cougar Edwards
PRO LINGUA ASSOCIATES
15 Elm Street, Brattleboro, Vermont 05301 USA 800-366-4775
Copyright © 1995 by Susannah J. Clark

Rabbit's Tail

Creek

Rabbit was hopping through a meadow one afternoon when suddenly Wildcat leaped and caught her. "I am going to eat you, Rabbit," Wildcat said.

"Please don't eat me, Wildcat," Rabbit begged. "I am small. If you let me go I will bring you Turkey, who is big and fat."

Wildcat decided to let Rabbit try. Rabbit told Wildcat to lie down in the meadow and pretend to be dead, and then Rabbit ran to find some turkeys.

Rabbit soon found them. "Wildcat is dead," Rabbit said. "Come see."

The turkeys went with Rabbit to the meadow. When they saw Wildcat lying on the ground, they began to dance and sing. "Wildcat is dead, Wildcat is dead," they sang.

Rabbit danced too, but Rabbit sang different words. "Jump up and catch the biggest," Rabbit sang.

The turkeys realized they had been tricked, but it was too late. Wildcat jumped up and grabbed the biggest turkey. Rabbit ran away, but the other turkeys chased Rabbit until one of them bit off Rabbit's long tail. Since that time Rabbit has only a short stub of a tail.

29 (S:15)

The Origin of Snakes

Taos

Once three women, Blue Corn, Yellow Corn, and Squawberry Flower, were all in love with the same man. When he decided to marry Squawberry Flower, the Corn women became very jealous. They invited the couple to their house for dinner. They sent the husband outside to bring in the turkey, but when he entered the house, he passed through a magic wheel the women had placed against the door, and he changed into a coyote. "Now you will live with us instead of Squawberry Flower," they said.

The coyote went to a shaman, who took out his own magic wheel. When the coyote passed through it, he changed back into a man.

The shaman gave the young man two magic arm bands. The man disguised himself and went to the house where the Corn women lived. He gave each of them an arm band, and when they put them on, they changed into snakes. "Because of your jealousy," the man told them, "you will crawl on the ground in the hot sun, and people will always despise you."

The man and Squawberry Flower lived happily, and they taught all their children not be jealous.

30 (S:13)

Seven Stars

Huron-Wyandot

There was an old woman who had seven sons. One day the boys played hard and became hungry. One of the boys went to the old woman and asked for some bread, but she did not give him any. "Stop bothering me and go back to your game!" she said. So the boy went back to his brothers and began to play again.

Soon another boy went to ask for bread, but the old woman sent him away, too. Each boy went, but all got the same answer.

Then one of the boys made a drum and the brothers began to dance. As they started dancing, they began to float up into the sky. The old woman looked up and saw what was happening. She grabbed a loaf of bread and ran to the boys, but it was too late. They continued dancing, and although she cried for them to eat, they rose higher and higher into the sky. She finally had to give up and cried for days over her lost sons.

Today the boys can still be seen in the sky. They are known as the Hutinatsija, the Cluster, seven stars in the sky.

31 (S:7,8)

Why Buffalo Went Away

Kiowa

Buffalo took good care of the Kiowa people. Everything the Kiowa had came from Buffalo. Their clothes came from Buffalo, their tipis came from Buffalo, and their food came from Buffalo. When the white men came to drive away the Kiowa, Buffalo tore up the railroads and farms built by the white men. So the white men declared war on Buffalo. They shot Buffalo's people, as many as a hundred in one day, and soon the prairie was covered with dead buffalos, and there were fewer and fewer of them to be found.

Buffalo saw he could no longer protect the Kiowa against the white men. He gathered together the last buffalos to decide what to do. The Kiowas who were still left were camped nearby, and early one morning, a young woman got up and went for a walk. She saw a mountain split open, and she saw Buffalo and his people walk straight into it. Inside the mountain she saw a green, fresh world. The rivers ran clear, not red, and flowers bloomed on the hillsides. The mountain closed behind Buffalo, and to this day, there are no more buffalos living in the Great Plain.

32 (S:12)

Why Bear Waddles

Comanche

STORY CARDS: NORTH AMERICAN INDIAN TALES
by Susannah J. Clark, illustrated by Ken Rainbow Cougar Edwards
PRO LINGUA ASSOCIATES
15 Elm Street, Brattleboro, Vermont 05301 USA 800-366-4775

The Origin of Arrowheads

Shasta

STORY CARDS: NORTH AMERICAN INDIAN TALES
by Susannah J. Clark, illustrated by Ken Rainbow Cougar Edwards
PRO LINGUA ASSOCIATES
15 Elm Street, Brattleboro, Vermont 05301 USA 800-366-4775
Copyright © 1995 by Susannah J. Clark

Why Mole Lives Underground

Cherokee

STORY CARDS: NORTH AMERICAN INDIAN TALES
by Susannah J. Clark, illustrated by Ken Rainbow Cougar Edwards
PRO LINGUA ASSOCIATES
15 Elm Street, Brattleboro, Vermont 05301 USA 800-366-4775
Copyright © 1995 by Susannah J. Clark

The Raven

Cree

STORY CARDS: NORTH AMERICAN INDIAN TALES
by Susannah J. Clark, illustrated by Ken Rainbow Cougar Edwards
PRO LINGUA ASSOCIATES
15 Elm Street, Brattleboro, Vermont 05301 USA 800-366-4775
Copyright © 1995 by Susannah J. Clark

The Origin of Arrowheads

Shasta

Long ago, humans used to hunt with arrows that had points made of pine bark. The arrows did not work very well, and the people often went hungry.

Ground Squirrel knew that Obsidian Man had arrowheads made of obsidian, and he decided to trade for some. He gathered a basket of roots and went to Obsidian Man's home. Obsidian Man told him, "I will give you all the arrowheads you want, but I must have more roots to eat."

Ground Squirrel went to gather more roots, but while he was filling his basket, Grizzly Bear came and sat on Ground Squirrel and ate all the roots.

Ground Squirrel crawled back to Obsidian Man and told him what had happened. The next day, when Ground Squirrel went again to dig more roots, Obsidian Man hid himself nearby. Again Grizzly Bear came and sat on Ground Squirrel, but when he reached for the roots, Obsidian Man killed him with an arrow.

Ground Squirrel thanked Obsidian Man, and they went home and ate the roots together. The next morning, Ground Squirrel gathered up as many of the arrowheads as he could. He carried them to the people, and that night there was a great feast.

Why Bear Waddles

Comanche

Once the animals who come out at night got into an argument with the animals who come out during the day. "We want it to be night all the time so we can go out whenever we want," they said. The animals who lived during the day said, "We want it to be day all the time."

The two groups of animals decided to play a guessing game. It was a long game. At first one side seemed to be winning, then the other side. It was such a long game that Bear became tired. He took off his moccasins to rest his feet a little.

Finally the sun began to come up, and the game still had not ended. The night animals played as long as they could, but finally it was too bright, and they all ran home. Bear, who had taken off his moccasins, put them on the wrong feet and forgot to tie the laces, so he waddled after the other animals in a funny, shuffling walk. "Wait for me!" he called, but they were in such a hurry to get home that they did not slow down. Bear waddled all the way home, and he still walks like that today.

The Raven

Cree

Once all the animals ate meat. Then the Great Spirit noticed that the number of animals was getting smaller, not larger. So He decided to change some of the animals' diets. He called all the animals together and asked them to stand in a line. Humans came first, and the Great Spirit decided they would eat plants and animals. Moose, who was next, got a diet of water plants and tree twigs.

A large black bird near the end of the line could not wait to find out what he would eat. He flew up to the front. "What am I going to eat?" he asked.

"Go back to your place in line and wait your turn," the Great Spirit said.

The bird returned to his place, but in a few minutes he was back. "What am I going to eat?" he asked again.

The Great Spirit was becoming angry. "Wait your turn, and you will find out!" He commanded.

The bird flew off, but soon he was back again, demanding, "What will I eat?"

The Great Creator lost His temper. "From this day, black bird, your name is Raven. You will eat only rotten, dead animals. You will be a thief, and only by stealing will you survive."

Why Mole Lives Underground

Cherokee

Once a man fell in love with a woman who would have nothing to do with him. The man became very unhappy, and could not eat or sleep because of his broken heart. The shamans tried to help the man, but there was nothing they could do to make the woman fall in love with him.

Mole heard about the man, and he went to the shamans. "I can help the man," he told them.

The shamans laughed. "We are old and wise, and we cannot help this man," they told him. "You are just a small animal. You cannot help. Go home."

Mole went to see the man anyway. "I know some magic," he said to the man. "I will help you." That night, as the woman slept, Mole sang a magic chant over her.

The next day, when the woman woke, all she could think about was the man. Finally she went to him and told him she loved him, and they were married.

The shamans heard about the marriage and wondered why the woman had changed her mind. When the man told them Mole had done it, the shamans were outraged and vowed to kill Mole because he had done what they could not. Because of that, Mole lives underground, hiding from the shamans.

How Buzzard Lost Its Voice

Pomo

STORY CARDS: NORTH AMERICAN INDIAN TALES
by Susannah J. Clark, illustrated by Ken Rainbow Cougar Edwards
PRO LINGUA ASSOCIATES
15 Elm Street, Brattleboro, Vermont 05301 USA 800-366-4775

Coyote Kills the Giant

Flathead

STORY CARDS: NORTH AMERICAN INDIAN TALES
by Susannah J. Clark, illustrated by Ken Rainbow Cougar Edwards
PRO LINGUA ASSOCIATES
15 Elm Street, Brattleboro, Vermont 05301 USA 800-366-4775
Copyright © 1995 by Susannah J. Clark

Wind

Micmac

STORY CARDS: NORTH AMERICAN INDIAN TALES
by Susannah J. Clark, illustrated by Ken Rainbow Cougar Edwards
PRO LINGUA ASSOCIATES
15 Elm Street, Brattleboro, Vermont 05301 USA 800-366-4775
Copyright © 1995 by Susannah J. Clark

Glooscap and the Baby

Algonquian

STORY CARDS: NORTH AMERICAN INDIAN TALES
by Susannah J. Clark, illustrated by Ken Rainbow Cougar Edwards
PRO LINGUA ASSOCIATES
15 Elm Street, Brattleboro, Vermont 05301 USA 800-366-4775
Copyright © 1995 by Susannah J. Clark

Coyote Kills the Giant

Flathead

Once there was a giant who ate all the animals and people he met. Coyote decided to stop the giant, and went to find him. Coyote came to a huge cave and went deep into the cave to a large room. Many people and animals were moaning in pain inside the room.

"What is the matter?" Coyote asked. "Are you sick?"

The people answered, "The giant ate us, and we are starving to death in his stomach."

Coyote realized that he was inside the giant. He decided to help the people escape. He went to the side of the cave, cut chunks of meat out of the giant with his knife, and fed them to the people. Then he found the giant's heart and cut it open. As the giant died, he opened his mouth, and Coyote led all the people and animals out. But with the giant's last breath, his teeth closed on Wood Tick, the last to escape. Coyote pulled hard and freed Wood Tick.

"Look at me!" the insect cried. "Now I am completely flat!"

"At least you are not dead," Coyote answered.

Wood Tick realized that Coyote was right, and that he should be glad to be alive. He said, "That is true, Coyote. I will get used to being flat." And he did.

37 (S:9)

How Buzzard Lost Its Voice

Pomo

Buzzard used to sing more beautifully than any other bird in the world. One day it was in the forest with its friends Hawk, Meadow Lark, and Squirrel. They all liked to talk, but they all talked at the same time, and no one could be heard. Finally Hawk said, "Let's see who can keep quiet the longest." Hawk and Buzzard were on one team, and Squirrel and Meadow Lark were on the other. The first animal to break the silence would lose its voice, and the other team would win the songs of the losing side.

The animals sat together in silence and made faces, trying to make each other laugh. Finally Buzzard could not help itself. It opened its beak to laugh–but no sound came out at all. It had lost its beautiful voice.

Squirrel cried, "We won! We won!" But it did not want to shame its friends Buzzard and Hawk. So Squirrel took only a small part of Buzzard's song. Hawk lost its voice even though it didn't laugh. But when Hawk opened its beak to complain, it could only whistle. Meadow Lark happily took the voices of Buzzard and Hawk, and to this day, Meadow Lark has three voices, but Buzzard, who was once the most beautiful singer in the world, has none.

38 (S:5

Glooscap and the Baby

Algonquian

Mighty Glooscap had beaten all the giants and the monsters. He told himself he was a very great man, and boasted to a woman that he could conquer everything.

The woman just laughed. "Are you sure? There is one creature no one will ever conquer."

Glooscap was surprised. "What is the name of this creature?"

"Wasis is his name," the woman told Glooscap, "but stay far away from him."

Wasis was the woman's baby, and he sat on the floor sucking a piece of maple sugar and singing a song. Glooscap did not know much about babies, so when he saw this small, sweet creature on the floor, he decided to ignore the woman's advice.

Glooscap smiled at Wasis. "Come to me," he told the baby. Wasis smiled back but never moved. Glooscap sang a beautiful birdsong, but Wasis just sucked on his maple sugar. Glooscap did not like to be ignored. He became very angry, and he shouted at Wasis, "Come to me!" Wasis began to cry and scream loudly. Glooscap shouted terrible threats, and jumped up and down and waved his fists. But Wasis just cried louder.

Finally Glooscap gave up and ran from the house. Wasis smiled and said, "Goo, goo!"

Today, when a baby smiles and says "Goo," it is remembering the time it conquered mighty Glooscap.

39 (S:9)

Wind

Micmac

Once the wind blew so hard that the Micmacs had to stay indoors. They could not fish for eels, and they became very hungry. Finally one young man went out to see if any fish had washed up on the shore. As he was out walking, he saw a big bird, the storm king, standing out on the rocks and flapping it wings. The man realized the bird was causing the wind, and h got an idea. "Grandfather," he called, "are you cold?"

"I am," the bird admitted.

"Let me carry you on my back over to the trees, where it is warmer," the man said, and the bird agreed. The bird climbed on the man's back, and the man began to cross the rocks back to the shore. Suddenly he pretended to slip. The bird fell off the man's back and broke one of his wings. The man bound up the bird's wing and told him to be still for several days.

The wind stopped blowing, and there was not even a breatl of air. The calm was so still that a scum formed on the ocean, and the Micmacs could not see to fish for eels. The man went back to the storm king. "Your wing is healed now, but you must be careful. Don't flap your wings too hard, or you will hurt yourself." And so there is wind, but not too much.

40 (S:1(

The Origin of the Sun

Cherokee

STORY CARDS: NORTH AMERICAN INDIAN TALES
by Susannah J. Clark, illustrated by Ken Rainbow Cougar Edwards
PRO LINGUA ASSOCIATES
15 Elm Street, Brattleboro, Vermont 05301 USA 800-366-4775

Why Crayfish Lives in Water

Seneca

STORY CARDS: NORTH AMERICAN INDIAN TALES
by Susannah J. Clark, illustrated by Ken Rainbow Cougar Edwards
PRO LINGUA ASSOCIATES
15 Elm Street, Brattleboro, Vermont 05301 USA 800-366-4775
Copyright © 1995 by Susannah J. Clark

Butterflies

Papago

STORY CARDS: NORTH AMERICAN INDIAN TALES
by Susannah J. Clark, illustrated by Ken Rainbow Cougar Edwards
PRO LINGUA ASSOCIATES
15 Elm Street, Brattleboro, Vermont 05301 USA 800-366-4775
Copyright © 1995 by Susannah J. Clark

How Fire Came to the Sierras

Concow Maidu

STORY CARDS: NORTH AMERICAN INDIAN TALES
by Susannah J. Clark, illustrated by Ken Rainbow Cougar Edwards
PRO LINGUA ASSOCIATES
15 Elm Street, Brattleboro, Vermont 05301 USA 800-366-4775
Copyright © 1995 by Susannah J. Clark

Why Crayfish Lives in Water

Seneca

Raccoon decided to play a trick on the crayfish, who lived on land then. He lay down and pretended to be dead. Soon a crayfish came along and saw Raccoon. Thinking his enemy was dead, he ran home and shouted, "Raccoon is dead! Raccoon is dead!"

The crayfish went to see Raccoon's body. When they saw it, they began to dance in a circle around the body. Suddenly, Raccoon jumped up and attacked the crayfish. Only one little crayfish escaped. He ran to a high mountain top.

Little Crayfish was very frightened because he did not know how to get home. He walked and walked and walked. He became so thirsty that he thought he was going to die. He asked a tree, "What kind of tree are you?"

The tree answered, "I am a black oak." Crayfish knew the black oak does not live near water. He was discouraged, but he crawled a bit further.

He asked another tree, "What kind of tree are you?"

"I am a cottonwood," the tree answered. Crayfish knew that cottonwood trees grow near water, so he kept going, and soon he came to another tree.

"What kind of a tree are you?" he asked.

"I am a willow," the tree answered. Crayfish knew that willows grow beside water, so he made one last, long jump and landed in a stream. He took such a long drink that he sank to the bottom, and he still lives there today.

41 (S:7)

The Origin of the Sun

Cherokee

Once all the animals lived in darkness. Every time they stumbled into each other, they said, "We need light." Finally they called a meeting. Redheaded Woodpecker told everyone, "I hear there is a land where the people have light every day."

The animals decided to send someone to that land to bring back some light. Possum said, "I will go." She walked west unt she came to the land of the sun. She took a piece of the sun an put it in the thick fur of her tail, but as she ran home, the sun burned off all the fur on Possum's tail and got away. Then Buzzard flew to the land of the sun. He took a piece of the sun and put it in the thick feathers on the top of his head, but as he flew home, the sun burned off all the feathers on Buzzard's head and got away.

The animals were afraid they would never have light, but the Spider spoke up. "I will help you," she said. Spider molded a clay bowl and, when it was dry, carried it to the land of the sun She took a piece of the sun, put it in the bowl, and carried it home. From then on everyone had sun.

Today, when people make pottery bowls, they still make them the way Spider did–they dry them slowly in the shade before they put them in the heat of the oven.

42 (S:1

How Fire Came to the Sierras

Concow Maidu

One day the animals were making acorn soup when they noticed smoke rising across the valley. They had never seen smoke before, so they decided to find out what it was. When they came near the smoke, they found a roundhouse guarded by birds. The door was open, and the animals saw a red creature dancing inside. They were so curious about the strange red thing that Coyote decided to steal it. But Mockingbird, who was watching for thieves, saw Coyote and screamed loudly. The other birds flew at Coyote and pecked him until he crawled away.

"No one can steal that creature," Coyote said to his friends. "Let's go home."

But Mouse, who was very small, crept into the roundhouse unseen. She took a coal from the fire, put it into her pack, and hurried back to her friends. They all looked at the glowing red coal in Mouse's pack, but when Coyote reached out to touch the coal, it burned his paw.

Coyote's yelps of pain caught Mockingbird's attention. Mockingbird saw what the animals had done and called the other birds, who began to chase them. Deer, who ran fastest, took the coal and held it between his hind legs. The coal scorched his fur, and that is why the rear legs of the Sierra deer are dark. When the animals got home, Deer dropped the coal on a pile of buckeye wood. The wood instantly caught fire, and that is how fire came to the Sierra people. Today, Maidu Indians still prefer buckeye for starting their fires.

43 (S:11)

Butterflies

Papago

The Creator watched a group of children playing with their puppies on a bright summer day. He was sad. "These children will grow old. Their hair will turn gray. Their teeth will fall out. Their skin will wrinkle. The puppies will become scrawny old dogs. The colors of the flowers will fade. The leaves from the trees will turn brown and dry up." The Creator became sadder and sadder.

But then He looked around at all the colors and got an idea. The Creator took out a bag and began collecting things: a spot of sunlight, a handful of blue from the sky, the green of the pine needles, and the red, orange, purple and yellow from the flowers. Finally He took the song of the birds and put that in the bag, too.

The Great Creator went to the children and gave the bag to them. "Little children, this is for you." When the children opened the bag, hundreds and hundreds of butterflies of every color flew out and landed on the grass, the trees, and the children's hair. The butterflie began to sing a beautiful song, and the children stopped to listen.

A songbird who had been flying past stopped, too. "Creator," the bird said, "You gave those songs to us birds when you made us. No You have also given them to these creatures. They already have all the colors of the rainbow. Isn't that enough?"

The Creator saw that the bird was right and took the songs away from the butterflies. And so today butterflies are beautiful, but they have no voices.

44 (S:9

The Origin of Corn

Seminole

STORY CARDS: NORTH AMERICAN INDIAN TALES
by Susannah J. Clark, illustrated by Ken Rainbow Cougar Edwards
PRO LINGUA ASSOCIATES
15 Elm Street, Brattleboro, Vermont 05301 USA 800-366-4775

How Mosquitoes Came to Be

Tlingit

STORY CARDS: NORTH AMERICAN INDIAN TALES
by Susannah J. Clark, illustrated by Ken Rainbow Cougar Edwards
PRO LINGUA ASSOCIATES
15 Elm Street, Brattleboro, Vermont 05301 USA 800-366-4775
Copyright © 1995 by Susannah J. Clark

How Crow Came to Be Black

Brule Sioux

STORY CARDS: NORTH AMERICAN INDIAN TALES
by Susannah J. Clark, illustrated by Ken Rainbow Cougar Edwards
PRO LINGUA ASSOCIATES
15 Elm Street, Brattleboro, Vermont 05301 USA 800-366-4775
Copyright © 1995 by Susannah J. Clark

Why Owl Has Big Eyes

Iroquois

STORY CARDS: NORTH AMERICAN INDIAN TALES
Σ by Susannah J. Clark, illustrated by Ken Rainbow Cougar Edwards
PRO LINGUA ASSOCIATES
15 Elm Street, Brattleboro, Vermont 05301 USA 800-366-4775
Copyright © 1995 by Susannah J. Clark

How Mosquitoes Came to Be

Tlingit

A long time ago, there was a giant who liked to kill people and drink their blood. The people got together to decide what to do about the monster. One man said, "I know how to kill the giant." He went to a path the giant often walked, and he lay down and pretended to be dead.

Soon the giant came along. He saw the man on the ground and said, "What a tasty meal!" The giant picked up the man and carried him home. He dropped the man on the floor and went outside to get some firewood. As soon as the giant was gone, the man jumped up and grabbed the giant's knife, which was lying on a table.

Just then the giant's son came in. The man held the knife to his throat. "Tell me, where is your father's heart?"

The giant's son was afraid. "It is in his left heel," he said.

The door opened, and the giant stepped into the room with his left foot first. Quickly the man stabbed the giant's heel, and the giant fell down dead.

The giant's son said, "You have killed my father, but he will keep eating people forever!"

"That's what you think," the man said. He cut the giant's body into pieces and burned each one of them in a fire. Then he took the ashes and threw them into the air.

But the giant's son was right. Each piece of ash turned into a mosquito, and the man suddenly felt a sting. The mosquito began sucking his blood, and the man began to scratch.

45 (S:9)

The Origin of Corn

Seminole

Once two young men lived with their grandmother. They were very good hunters, and they always had plenty of meat, but one day they said they were not happy.

"What is the matter?" the grandmother asked.

"We are tired of meat," one of the men said. "We want something new."

"When you come home, I will have something for you," she said.

The men hunted all day and found a deer. When they brought it home, they smelled something delicious. When they sat down to ea they could not believe how delicious the new food was. "It is called corn," the grandmother said, "and everything you eat will taste bett with it."

The men wondered where the corn had come from. The next da they hid behind a tree to watch. At noon the grandmother came ou of the house, drew a circle in the dirt and sat down in it. She sang a song and rubbed her hands against her sides, and corn fell off.

That night the two men were not very hungry. The grandmother guessed what had happened. "You have found out my secret," she told them. "It is time for me to leave you. When I am dead, bury my body and carefully tend the plants that grow from it. They will be corn plants, and if you take care of them and save some of the seed every year to plant in the spring, you will always have plenty of corn

The men were very sad to lose their grandmother, but they did a she asked, and that is how corn came to be.

46 (S:1

Why Owl Has Big Eyes

Iroquois

The Creator was making the animals. It was Rabbit's turn. "I want to have long legs and ears like Deer's and sharp teeth and claws like Panther's," Rabbit said. The Creator began shaping long legs for Rabbit.

Owl was waiting to be made. "Whoo, whoo!" Owl screeched. "I want a beautiful long neck like Swan's, and bright red feathers like Cardinal's, and a long beak like Egret's, and a crown of feathers on my head like Heron. I want to be the most beautiful, the fastest, and the best of all the birds."

The Creator did not want to be bothered. "Be quiet and look the other way. No one is allowed to watch me work."

But Owl did not listen. "Whoo, whoo! I like to watch you work, so I will."

The Creator became angry and grabbed Owl. He pushed Owl's head down tight onto his shoulders and rubbed Owl in mud. He shook Owl until his eyes grew big with fright, and pulled on Owl's ears until they stuck up in the air. "That will teach you," said the Creator. "Now you have big ears to hear when someone tells you what to do. Now you have big eyes to see—but you will not be able to watch me, because you will sleep during the day. Your feathers will be gray like mud."

Owl flew away, pouting, and the Creator turned back to finish making Rabbit. But Rabbit had run away, even though he was not finished. So today Rabbit has long ears, but only half of Rabbit's legs are long like deer's, so he has to hop everywhere he goes. And because he did not get sharp teeth and claws, Rabbit is afraid of almost everything.

47 (S:9)

How Crow Came to Be Blac

Brule Sioux

A long time ago, when Crow was white, people depended on the buffal for food. But Crow was a friend of the buffalo, and whenever Crow saw hunters coming, he cried, "Caw, caw! The hunters are coming!" The buffalo would stampede, and the people went hungry.

The people held a meeting to decide what to do. One wise old man suggested, "We must capture Crow and teach him a lesson." He brough out a buffalo skin and put it on the back of a young hunter. "Nephew," l said, "sneak in among the buffalo, and you will be able to capture Crow.

The young hunter did as he was told. He crept into the buffalo herd, and the other hunters marched from their camp toward the herd. Crow saw this and flew to warn the buffalo. "Caw, caw! The hunters are near!" All the buffalo stampeded away—except for the young hunter hidden under the buffalo skin, who pretended to go on eating grass.

Crow flew down and sat on the young hunter's shoulder. "Caw, caw! Are you deaf? The hunters are near! Save yourself!" The young hunter grabbed Crow. The bird tried to escape, but the young hunter held him and tied him up.

The people took Crow back to their camp. "What are we going to do with Crow?" they asked. The young hunter grabbed the bird. "Let's bur Crow!" He pushed Crow into the fire. The string that tied Crow burned up at once, and the bird flew away. But the fire had burned Crow's feathers, and they were no longer white.

So Crow escaped, and after that, the buffalo hunt got a little bit easier because Crow never again tried to warn the buffalo. But Crow has been black ever since.

48 (S: